To all the people I've met on this beautiful island, thank you for the inspiration.

Text by Brooke Dean
Illustrations by Corryn Webb

ISBN: 979-8-9876901-3-0

Published in Tallassee, Alabama
Printed in the United States of America.
Library of Congress Control Number:2024920799

First printing edition 2024

Edited by Robin Katz
Cover design and typesetting by Ryan Webb

Bon Voyage Books

K is for Kwajalein

A Marshall Islands Alphabet Book

WRITTEN BY
BROOKE DEAN

ILLUSTRATED BY
CORRYN WEBB

Letter A stands for **ATOLLS:**
Reefs in the Pacific.

And B is for **Bikes**—
So unique and terrific!

Now, **C** stands for **COCONUTS.**
Crabs, too, you'll see.

And then **D** is for **DIVERS**
deep down in the sea.

Letter **E** stands for **EMON BeaCH.**
Kids love to play there,

while **F** is for **FERRIES**
that make water spray there!

Well, **G** stands for **GOLF CARTS** with festive décor.

You'll see **H** is for **HOBBY SHOPS**:
Find art galore!

Letter I stands for **ISLAND**

with palm trees and shells.

Also, **J** is for sea **JEWELRY**
each merchant sells.

And then **L** is for **LEMONADE.**
Drink some . . . Then roam!

MARSHALL ISLANDS has M.
Flags have WHITE / ORANGE / BLUE.

We know **N** is for **NEIGHBORS.**
Hello! How are *you?*

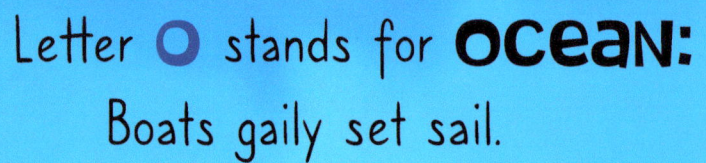

Letter **o** stands for **ocean:**
Boats gaily set sail.

Clearly, **P** is for **PLANES**
bringing food, treats, and mail.

Letter Q stands for **QUIET:**
We'll watch the sun rise.

Likewise, **R** is for **REEFS**

which the sea creatures prize.

Letter **S** stands for **SUNSETS** of **PINK**-**PURPLE** hue.

Know that **T** is for **TIDE POOL:**
Sea creatures, we'll view!

Think of **U: UNDERWATER,**

we snorkel near ships.

Often, **v** is for **VICTORY**
CHEERS on our lips!

WATER POLO with W—
Swimming and chasing.

And X is for **exercise:**
Go, Rustman Racing!

Yes, Y is for **YELLOW,**
the shine of the sun.

You'll find **z** is for **zest:**
Celebrations and fun!

You have seen **KWAJALEIN,** now—
from **A** down through **Z.**

Come and visit this haven
way out in the sea!

ABOUT THE AUTHOR

Brooke Dean's life has been full of amazing adventures on the beautiful island of Kwajalein Atoll (also called Kwaj) since moving there in July 2022. Currently, she loves teaching third-grade students there . . . as well as writing and illustrating unique books for kids!

Brooke hopes that her rhyming book about exploring Kwajalein from A to Z will give readers a taste of everything that magical place has to offer. She takes this opportunity to extend to her readers the friendly Kwaj greeting, **"Iokwe!"** (pronounced YOK-way).

That's the Marshallese version of **'HELLO!'**

Kwaj weekend activities that Brooke especially enjoys include boat trips to Bigej Island, beachcombing for sea glass and shells, snorkeling the tide pools, and floating at Emon beach.

The yearly winter holiday activities on Kwaj are some of Brooke's favorite island events. There are always unusual seasonal celebrations, such as the Golf Cart Christmas Parade and the palm tree lighting with a snow machine. There's even a Scuba Santa!

Are you ready to discover Kwajalein Island from A to Z? Begin on the first page, and off we'll go!